GW01271342

STYLE IT OUT

Welcome to the world of Harry Styles, home to record-breaking smash hits, best-selling albums, pioneering fashion statements and silver screen appearances. Whether you were there way back in 2010, when five young lads competing on *The X Factor* combined forces to become one of the most successful boy bands in history, or your first experience of Harry was a serious hit of 'Watermelon Sugar', there is something for every Styler out there. From his early days in One Direction to his big screen breakthrough in *Dunkirk* and his Grammy-winning solo work, prepare yourself for a journey into a career that, once begun, was never going to leave the music world as it was. Lights up!

THE ULTIMATE FAN'S GUIDE TO
HARRY STYLES

Future PLC Quay House, The Ambury, Bath, BA1 1UA

Editorial
Editor **Charles Ginger**
Senior Art Editor **Andy Downes**
Head of Art & Design **Greg Whitaker**

Editorial Director **Jon White**

Contributors
Neil Crossley, Bee Ginger, Alice Pattilo, Drew Sleep, Henry Yates

Cover images
Getty Images

Photography
All images © Getty, Alamy
All copyrights and trademarks are recognised and respected

Advertising
Media packs are available on request
Commercial Director **Clare Dove**

International
Head of Print Licensing **Rachel Shaw**
licensing@futurenet.com
www.futurecontenthub.com

Circulation
Head of Newstrade **Tim Mathers**

Production
Head of Production **Mark Constance**
Production Project Manager **Matthew Eglinton**
Advertising Production Manager **Joanne Crosby**
Digital Editions Controller **Jason Hudson**
Production Managers **Keely Miller, Nola Cokely,
Vivienne Calvert, Fran Twentyman**

Printed in the UK

Distributed by Marketforce, 5 Churchill Place, Canary Wharf, London, E14 5HU
www.marketforce.co.uk Tel: 0203 787 9001

Ultimate Fan's Guide To Harry Styles (MUB4757)
© 2022 Future Publishing Limited

Connectors.
Creators.
Experience
Makers.

Future plc is a public
company quoted on the
London Stock Exchange
(symbol: FUTR)
www.futureplc.com
Tel +44 (0)1225 442 244

Widely
Recycled

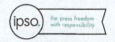

ipso
For press freedom
with responsibility

Chief executive **Zillah Byng-Thorne**
Non-executive chairman **Richard Huntingford**
Chief financial officer **Penny Ladkin-Brand**

RISING STAR

Sixteen-year-old Harry Styles joins his bandmates in a London HMV store during the seventh series of *The X Factor*. Harry later revealed he had only attended the show's heats in 2010 because his mother had signed him up. "I went to the audition to find out if I could sing," he later told Hamish Bowles in an interview for *Vogue*, "or if my mum was just being nice to me." As a solo performer Harry was eliminated from the show, but he returned as one-fifth of One Direction (whose name he suggested), and the rest is pop history.

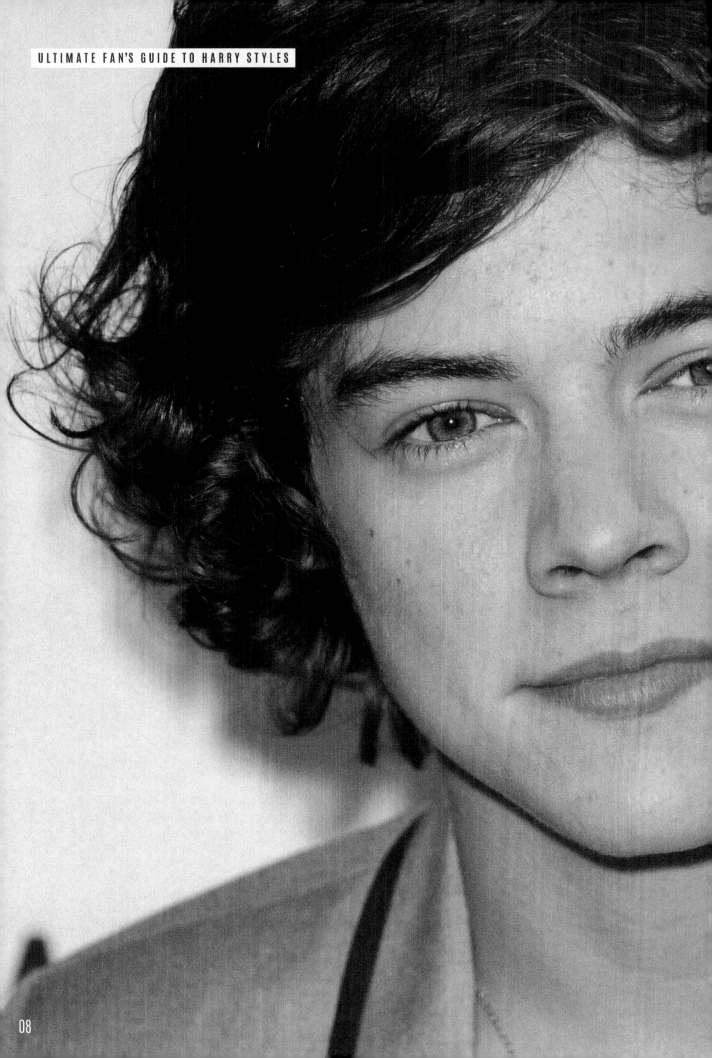

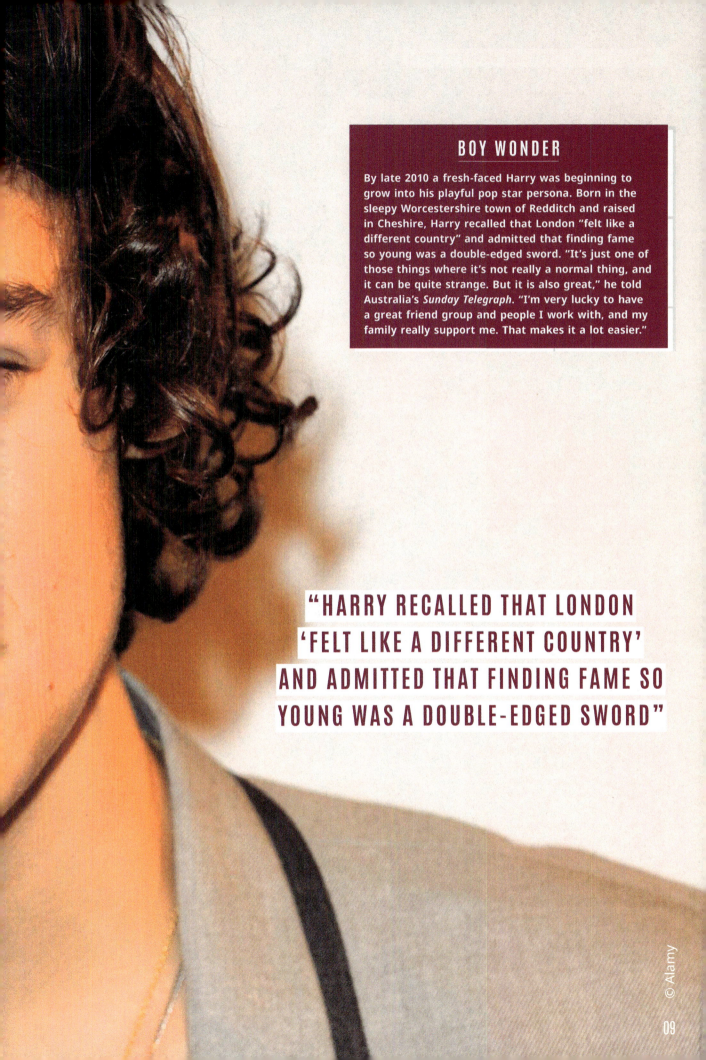

BOY WONDER

By late 2010 a fresh-faced Harry was beginning to grow into his playful pop star persona. Born in the sleepy Worcestershire town of Redditch and raised in Cheshire, Harry recalled that London "felt like a different country" and admitted that finding fame so young was a double-edged sword. "It's just one of those things where it's not really a normal thing, and it can be quite strange. But it is also great," he told Australia's *Sunday Telegraph.* "I'm very lucky to have a great friend group and people I work with, and my family really support me. That makes it a lot easier."

"HARRY RECALLED THAT LONDON 'FELT LIKE A DIFFERENT COUNTRY' AND ADMITTED THAT FINDING FAME SO YOUNG WAS A DOUBLE-EDGED SWORD"

A BREAK FROM REHEARSALS

The One Direction boys are pictured here taking a break from rehearsals at a recording studio in Battersea, London, on 18 October 2010. At the time *The X Factor* was undoubtedly one of the biggest programmes on TV, with a prime-time slot and almost a third of the UK population tuning in. The show's seventh season was a highly controversial spectacle, from the initial auditions to boot camp and even the live shows. One Direction's fellow contestants spoke warmly of the boys, saying they were great fun to be around, but they did admit that the green room would be left in chaos if 1D had been in there.

"ONE DIRECTION'S FELLOW CONTESTANTS SPOKE WARMLY OF THE BOYS, SAYING THEY WERE GREAT FUN TO BE AROUND"

© Getty

11

"HARRY AND ONE DIRECTION BANDMATES LIAM PAYNE, LOUIS TOMLINSON, ZAYN MALIK AND NIALL HORAN PREPARE TO STEP INTO POP HISTORY"

X MEN

At the press conference ahead of *The X Factor*'s live finals on 11 and 12 December 2010, Harry and One Direction bandmates Liam Payne, Louis Tomlinson, Zayn Malik and Niall Horan prepare to step into pop history. Looking back, it's baffling that despite show-stopping performances of Elton John's 'Your Song', Robbie Williams' 'She's The One' and Natalie Imbruglia's 'Torn', the band would have to be satisfied with third place, trailing behind that year's competition winner Matt Cardle and runner-up Rebecca Ferguson. 1D's mentor Simon Cowell later remembered that hearing the result was "like being punched in my stomach".

RED CARPET TREATMENT

On 30 November 2010, the One Direction boys attended the Royal Film Performance and world premiere of *The Chronicles Of Narnia: The Voyage Of The Dawn Treader*, based on the outstanding writings of C.S. Lewis, British lay theologian and writer. Here they are pictured arriving at London's Leicester Square Odeon Cinema. Despite the cold weather, they were joined by Simon Pegg, Liam Neeson and Joe McElderry, who had won *The X Factor* the previous year. Joe even performed a song from the film's soundtrack at the gala later that evening. Proceeds from the event went to the Cinema And Television Benevolent Fund. Her Majesty the Queen was also in attendance and even donned her 3D glasses to enjoy the film!

15

HIGH FLYERS

One Direction chartered a luxury helicopter to promote their debut single, 'What Makes You Beautiful', in September 2011. The song would prove a major springboard for the band, sparking the most pre-orders in Sony history, debuting in the UK at #1 and even scaling the US Billboard chart (where it peaked at #4). Even the high-brow music press got onboard. "The real genius is that the chord progression is simple enough to be played on an acoustic guitar at a house party," wrote *NME*'s Ailbhe Malone. "A tenner says this is 'our song' to four new pubescent couples by the end of the week."

CAN YOU MAKE IT OUT TO...

The One Direction boys in Manchester, England, to promote their new book *One Direction: Forever Young: Our Official X-Factor Story* at the local HMV store. Baby-faced and blushing, the boys were mobbed by fans young and old who had turned out in their masses to meet them and buy their first book. Hysterical diehards had queued overnight in the hope of getting one of the 500 coveted wristbands promising them access to the event and their idols. Those who didn't get into the venue on Market Street surrounded the building, ever hopeful of catching a glimpse of the famous five. Shoppers and onlookers were serenaded with ear-piercing screams from the crowd, which became deafening when the superstars arrived. Locals were particularly delighted to see Harry, who hails from nearby Holmes Chapel.

"THE BOYS WERE MOBBED BY FANS YOUNG AND OLD WHO HAD TURNED OUT IN THEIR MASSES TO MEET THEM"

SIGNED, SEALED, DELIVERED

One Direction oversee the shipment of their debut album, *Up All Night*, at Amazon's Marston Gate Fulfilment Centre on 21 November 2011. Led out by the all-conquering first single 'What Makes You Beautiful', the album would go on to sell 4.5 million copies worldwide and top the charts in 16 countries – even if it was held off the UK top spot by Rihanna's *Talk That Talk*. As Harry recalled in *Dazed*, all he could do was hang on tight and enjoy the ride. "I was sixteen. I'd just kind of finished school. Everything was really new and exciting, and I didn't know how long everything was gonna last."

21

HAVING YOUR CAKE

Grinning from behind a mask of red-and-blue icing, Harry accompanies his 1D bandmates during a 2012 appearance on the *Elvis Duran Show* in New York. On a global tour at the time, the band discussed how they formed, dating fans, and what exactly made them so successful, to which Harry replied, "I think what people like is that we don't have to try to get on. We just naturally get on. We're like the boys you went to school with. We're the boys who pick up the bras that are thrown on stage." After the show Harry was presented with a Union Jack-themed ice cream cake before his bandmates plunged him head-first into it. When returning to the show in 2017, Harry joked, "It was solid. It really hurt my nose."

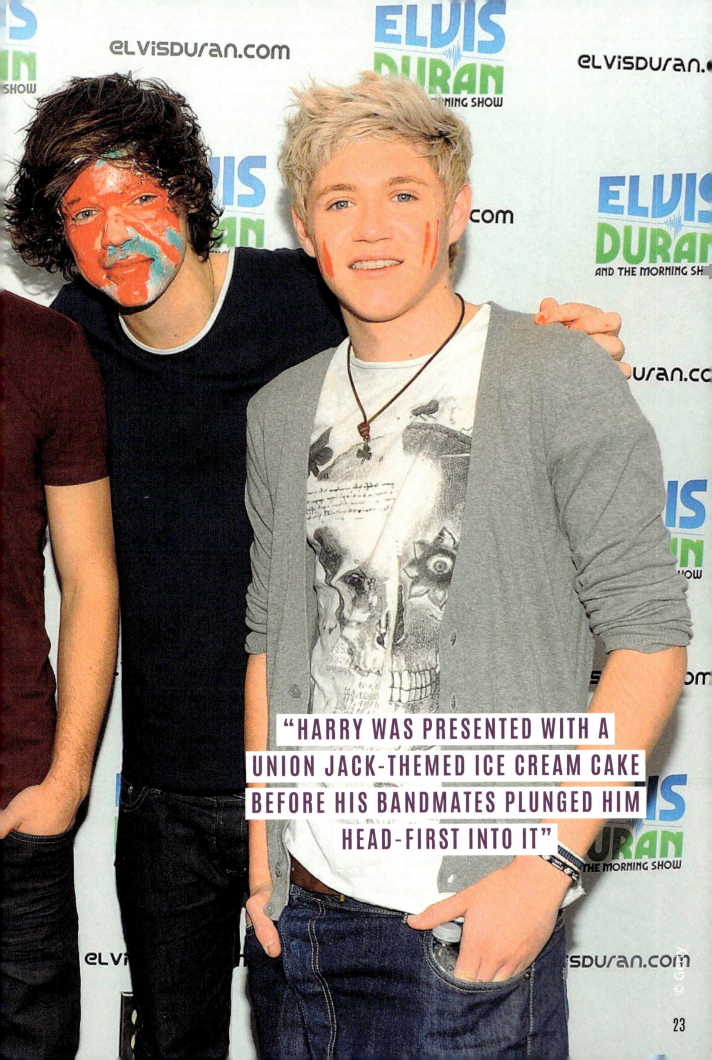

"HARRY WAS PRESENTED WITH A UNION JACK-THEMED ICE CREAM CAKE BEFORE HIS BANDMATES PLUNGED HIM HEAD-FIRST INTO IT"

STATESIDE SUPERSTARS

One Direction did not disappoint when they performed on NBC's popular morning television show *Today*, which was filmed on 13 November 2012 at the Rockefeller Plaza in New York City. The band were over in the US to promote the release of their second album, *Take Me Home*, from which they performed six songs to crowds of over 15,000 fans. Three songs aired during that morning's show: 'What Makes You Beautiful', 'Little Things' and 'Live While We're Young'. The other three tunes, 'One Thing', 'Moments' and 'Kiss You', were saved for the following day's show. Outside of the studio, the plaza had been turned into a full stage, complete with red-and-white candy-striped flooring and full-sized British red telephone boxes.

LIFE ON THE SILVER SCREEN

One Direction pose for photographers at the *This Is Us* world premiere at the Ziegfield Theater in New York City. Fans brought the busy Midtown streets to a standstill as they queued waiting for a sighting of their idols, with some even camping out overnight to catch a glimpse. Many stars, including Perez Hilton and Stephen Baldwin, took to the black carpet to enjoy the event. The 3D documentary concert film follows the boys on their *Take Me Home* Tour, giving an intimate insight into preparation for concerts as well as footage of their stratospheric rise from *The X Factor* to global music domination. The film was a huge success and grossed an impressive $68 million worldwide.

BRITISH INVASION

One Direction show off their trophy haul during the 2014 American Music Awards at Los Angeles' Nokia Theatre on 23 November. With wins for Artist Of The Year, Favourite Pop Group and Favourite Pop Album (for *Midnight Memories*), the band were now a force to be reckoned with – even if much of the press attention was focused on Harry's choice of headwear. "He's like a cute little Pilgrim, or a young Johnny Depp without the eyeliner," wrote *Cosmopolitan*. "Even if you don't condone male usage of hats, it's hard to deny that this was a good look for Mr Styles."

"WITH WINS FOR ARTIST OF THE YEAR, FAVOURITE POP GROUP AND FAVOURITE POP ALBUM, THE BAND WERE NOW A FORCE TO BE RECKONED WITH"

THEIR REIGN IN SPAIN

Sporting two awards, One Direction attend the 40 Principales Awards 2014 in Madrid, Spain. Hosted by the Los 40 Principales radio show, the event has proved a successful hunting ground for the band, with seven nominations and four wins. As well as performing 'Steal My Girl' at the 2014 edition, the group won Best International Act and Best International Video for 'Story Of My Life' while also being nominated for Best International Album for *Midnight Memories* (the best-selling album globally in 2013) only to lose out to Ed Sheeran's *X*. Previously they had bagged awards for Best International New Artist in 2012 and Best International Album for *Take Me Home* a year later.

"WOULD ANYONE MIND GRABBING ME SOME WINGS FROM HOOTERS?"

STREET PARTY

A four-piece One Direction take over Hollywood Boulevard for their November 2015 performance on *Jimmy Kimmel Live*. Promoting their fifth and (for now) final album, *Made In The A.M.*, the band aired new songs including 'Drag Me Down' and 'Love You Goodbye', while Harry's banter with the crowd was charmingly cheeky ("Would anyone mind grabbing me some wings from Hooters?" he asked at one point). The only sour note was the band's imminent hiatus. "After five years of non-stop grinding, they can't be blamed for wanting to disappear," wrote the *Los Angeles Times*. "But that doesn't mean they won't be missed."

33

LAST STAND

One Direction – minus Zayn Malik – attend the American Music Awards in Los Angeles on 22 November 2015. The band would go on to win Artist Of The Year for a second consecutive year, but the end was near. In an interview with *Rolling Stone*, Harry revealed he was the one to suggest the following year's hiatus. "I didn't want to exhaust our fanbase. If you're shortsighted, you can think, 'Let's just keep touring', but we all thought too much of the group than to let that happen. You realise you're exhausted and you don't want to drain people's belief in you."

HAPPY NEW YEAR!

In what would prove to be One Direction's final US TV appearance before their hiatus, Harry Styles whips up the crowd during the Billboard Hollywood Party on New Year's Eve 2015. Hosted in Los Angeles, the party was beamed across the US as part of *Dick Clark's New Year's Rockin' Eve with Ryan Seacrest 2016*, which is regularly the most-watched New Year's Eve special broadcast in America. Harry and his bandmates were attending the party for the second year in a row, this time as the headline act.

"IN ONE DIRECTION'S FINAL US TV APPEARANCE BEFORE THEIR HIATUS, HARRY WHIPS UP THE CROWD DURING THE BILLBOARD HOLLYWOOD PARTY"

© Getty

A MODEL PERFORMANCE

As supermodel Candace Swanepoel waltzes off the runway sporting an elaborate feathered costume Harry raises the roof with a superb rendition of 'Golden' at the 2017 Victoria's Secret Fashion Show in Shanghai, China. Held at the Mercedes-Benz Arena, the lingerie and sleepware brand's multi-million-dollar annual event hosted 18,000 attendees and was watched by 4.98 million viewers on CBS. They were all treated to a spectacular extravaganza that featured a typically mercurial performance by Harry, who also sang 'She' as a seemingly endless stream of models paraded by. Tough work, but somebody had to do it.

"THEY WERE TREATED TO A TYPICALLY MERCURIAL PERFORMANCE BY HARRY"

© Getty

39

DOMINATING DOWN UNDER

Harry thanks the crowd as he accepts the award for Best International Act at the 2017 Australian Recording Industry Association (ARIA) Awards in Sydney, Australia, at which he also performed 'Kiwi'. A prize voted for by the public, Harry beat the likes of Adele, Ed Sheeran, Bruno Mars and The Weeknd to clinch the award. He would repeat the feat in 2020, fending off Justin Bieber, Halsey and none other than ex-girlfriend Taylor Swift to win his second (to date) ARIA title. At the time of writing Harry, as a solo artist, has been nominated for 121 awards, winning 43 of them.

"ALREADY THE SOLO STAR HAD THE CHARISMA TO CARRY THE SHOW AND ONLY MISSED THE MARK WITH HIS FACE-PLANTING STAGE DIVE"

SOLO STAR

Harry performs at an iHeartRadio launch party on 8 May 2017 to celebrate the release of his debut solo record. Taking the stage at Brooklyn's iconic Rough Trade record store, the singer kicked off his set with a modest intro ("I'm Harry, nice to meet you") and a powerful rendition of 'Ever Since New York'. Already the solo singer had the charisma to carry the show and only missed the mark with his face-planting attempt at a stage dive. "I thought it'd feel like flying," he told *The Late Late Show With James Corden*, "but it was kind of like a sink hole."

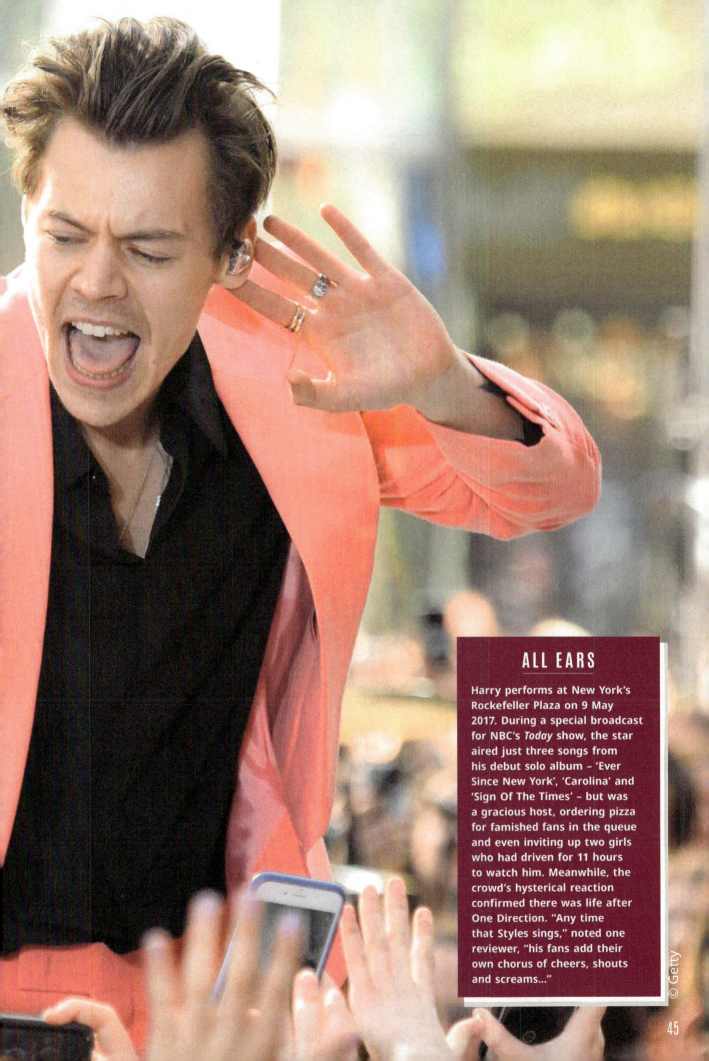

ALL EARS

Harry performs at New York's Rockefeller Plaza on 9 May 2017. During a special broadcast for NBC's *Today* show, the star aired just three songs from his debut solo album – 'Ever Since New York', 'Carolina' and 'Sign Of The Times' – but was a gracious host, ordering pizza for famished fans in the queue and even inviting up two girls who had driven for 11 hours to watch him. Meanwhile, the crowd's hysterical reaction confirmed there was life after One Direction. "Any time that Styles sings," noted one reviewer, "his fans add their own chorus of cheers, shouts and screams…"

© Getty

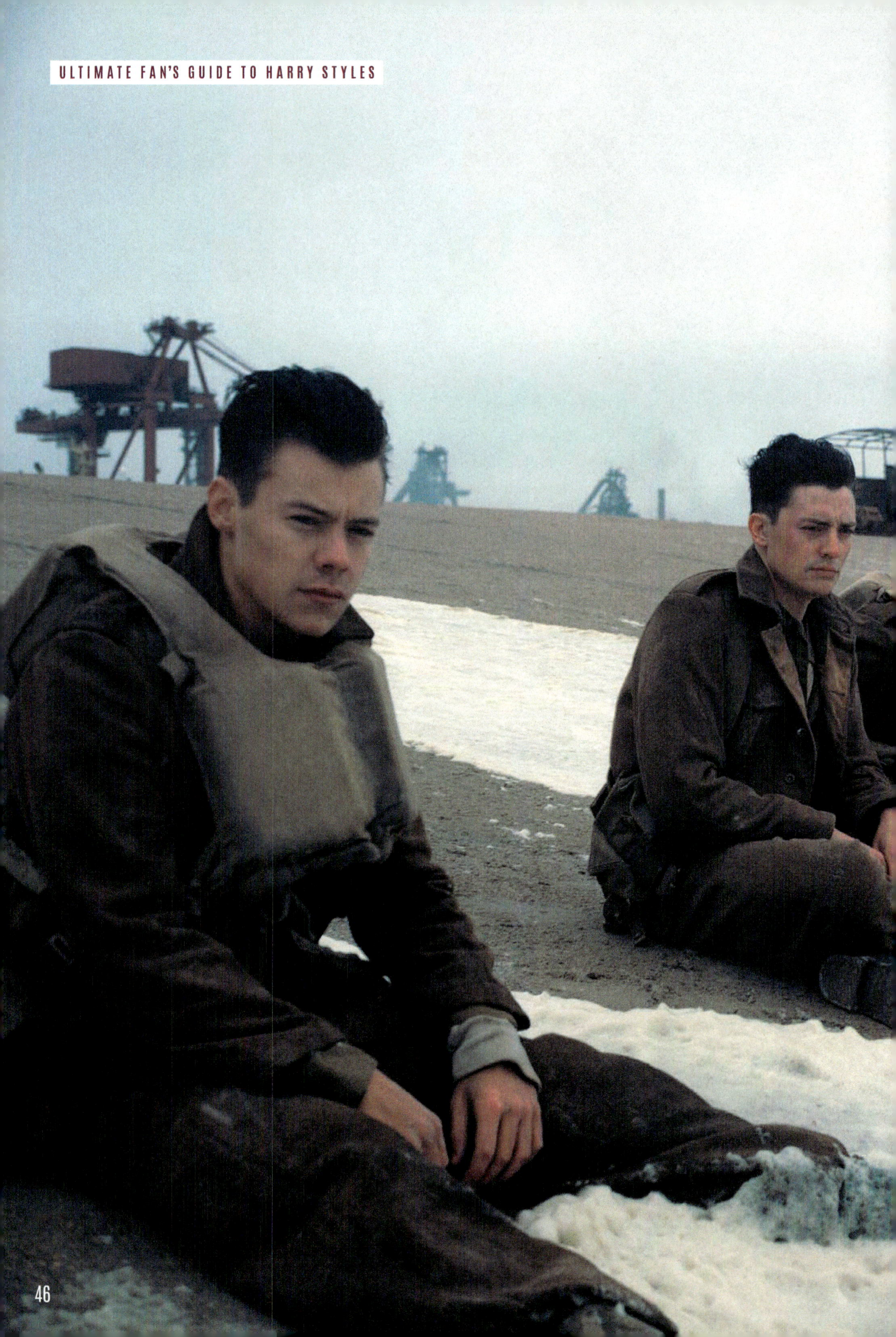

AGAINST ALL ODDS

In 2017 Harry made his acting debut in WWII blockbuster *Dunkirk*. Working alongside Aneurin Barnard and Fionn Whitehead, he played an ordinary British soldier marooned on Dunkirk's beaches after becoming surrounded by the advancing German army. Winston Churchill called it a "colossal military disaster" at the time, but the evacuation of over 338,000 Allied troops in the summer of 1940 by a hastily assembled fleet would prove to be a turning point. The film's director Christopher Nolan said he cast Styles "because he fit the part wonderfully and truly earned a seat at the table". *The Daily Telegraph* film critic Robbie Collin praised Styles for a "bright, convicted, and unexpectedly not-at-all-jarring performance".

"DESPITE NEVER ACTING IN A FEATURE FILM BEFORE, HE BEAT THOUSANDS OF ACTORS TO WIN THE ROLE OF ALEX"

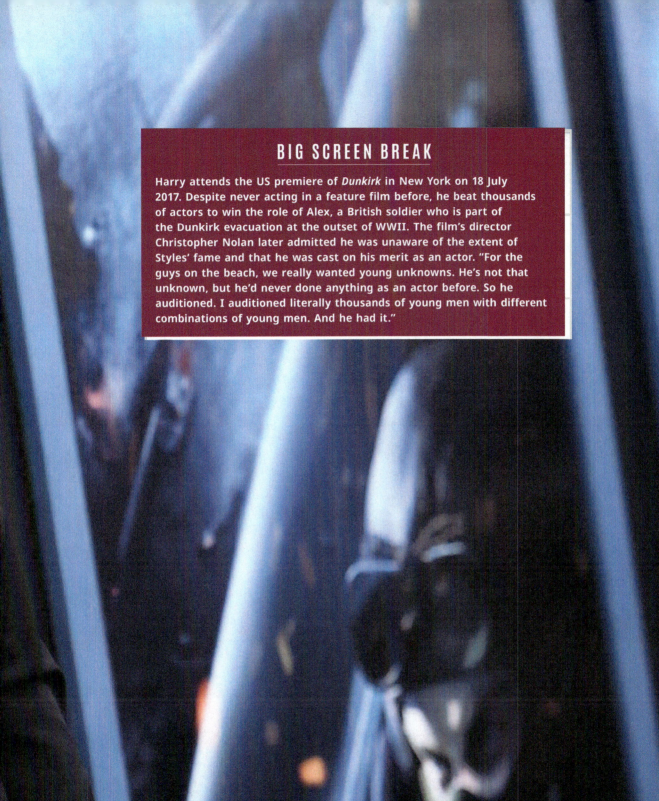

BIG SCREEN BREAK

Harry attends the US premiere of *Dunkirk* in New York on 18 July 2017. Despite never acting in a feature film before, he beat thousands of actors to win the role of Alex, a British soldier who is part of the Dunkirk evacuation at the outset of WWII. The film's director Christopher Nolan later admitted he was unaware of the extent of Styles' fame and that he was cast on his merit as an actor. "For the guys on the beach, we really wanted young unknowns. He's not that unknown, but he'd never done anything as an actor before. So he auditioned. I auditioned literally thousands of young men with different combinations of young men. And he had it."

DUNKIRK WORLD PREMIERE

The Odeon Leicester Square was the venue for the world premiere of Christopher Nolan's epic war film *Dunkirk* in July 2017. A Spitfire aircraft flanked the entrance and added a real dynamism to the premiere, at which Styles, Kenneth Branagh, Cillian Murphy, Tom Hardy and director Chrisopher Nolan walked the red carpet and stood in line to greet Prince Harry. All the actors paid tribute to the vision and unique talent of director Nolan. "Any time you get to work with someone who is so passionate about what they do," said Styles, "that's a privilege in itself."

"THERE'S MORE ROOM ON STAGE. THERE'S MORE WORDS THAT I HAVE TO REMEMBER. BUT IT'S BEEN REALLY FUN"

SUITS YOU

Wearing a flamboyant Gucci suit, Harry shows off his guitar skills during a September 2017 performance at Las Vegas' iHeartRadio Music Festival. The singer's five-song show leaned hard on his debut album, including 'Carolina', 'Two Ghosts', 'Only Angel', 'Sign Of The Times' and 'Kiwi', and the critics were impressed, with *Riff* magazine praising a "gutsy set" that "did much to leave his boy band past behind him." As for Harry, he was starting to recognise the pros and cons of going solo. "There's more room on stage," he considered in a backstage interview. "There's more words that I have to remember. But it's been really fun."

© Getty

A SWIFT RELATIONSHIP

Seen here together walking through New York's Central Park in the winter of 2012, Taylor Swift and Harry may only have dated for a few months, but their short-lived fling would have a huge impact on their musical careers. The superstar pair began their brief relationship in November 2013 after Harry pursued the country singer, but they would end up separating by March of the following year after a volcanic row while vacationing on the British Virgin Isles with the likes of Richard Branson. The pair subsequently referenced their relationship and break-up in their respective work, but despite the fact they didn't work out, there doesn't seem to be any animosity between them, as evidenced by Swift's genuine delight at Harry winning a Grammy in 2019 for his smash hit 'Watermelon Sugar'.

TEEN CHOICE

2013

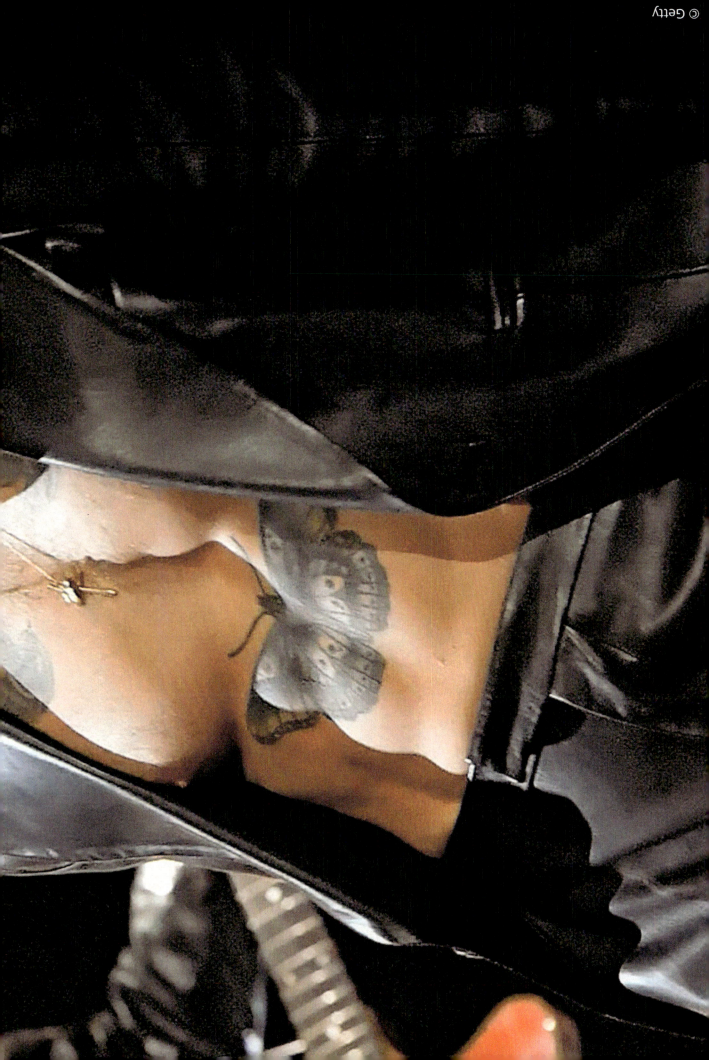

THE PROMISE OF A HERO

As the credits rolled at the end of *Eternals* few viewers expected the black and scrolling white to be interrupted by a mid-credits scene featuring a previously unheralded character, let alone one played by Harry Styles. But this is exactly what audiences got in 2021 when, following an intoxicated introduction from his elfish sidekick, Pip, Harry, or rather Eros, brother of Thanos, strolled onto the screen with a promise to help Angelina Jolie's Thena locate her endangered friends, strongly suggesting that the former One Direction frontman will soon be appearing for more than a few minutes in a new Marvel movie.

© Getty

ETERNALS

MOVING ON UP

Five dates into his triumphant Live On Tour run, Harry reaches New York's historic Radio City Music Hall on 28 September 2017. Opened in 1932 and nicknamed the 'showplace of the nation', the venue has hosted flagship industry events from the Grammys to the VMAs, but the singer never seemed overawed by the occasion. "My name is Harry, I'm from England," the singer told the crowd. "My job for the next hour and a little bit is to entertain you." According to *Billboard*'s review, the star didn't let them down: "He appeared exceedingly comfortable, pacing from end to end while rallying for more cheers…"

"STYLES LOOKED RELAXED, RELISHING THE COMEDIC POTENTIAL OF THE MOMENT AS HE ANNOUNCED THE BIRTH"

STANDING IN YOUR SHOES

The audience at the CBS Television City studios in Los Angeles erupted with applause when Harry Styles emerged from a giant stage curtain and walked out onto the studio floor to present *The Late Late Show With James Corden* on Tuesday 12 December 2017. Styles had been rushed to the studio to guest host the show when his good friend Corden joined his wife Jules at hospital for the birth of their daughter. Styles looked wholly relaxed in his new role, seemingly relishing the comedic potential of the moment as he announced the birth of the couple's baby girl. "I was actually just at the hospital and she looks a lot like James," grinned Styles, "mainly because James looks like a giant baby."

© Getty

67

STARS AND STRIPES

Harry performs on *The Late Late Show With James Corden* in May 2017. During a week-long residency in Los Angeles, the singer aired songs from his new self-titled debut solo album, as well as getting involved with the show's traditional stunts and sketches – including a game of Flinch that saw Harry attempting to drink a cup of tea while being pelted with fruit. Less well-received were the singer's attempts at fronting the show. "Styles gave a deadpan monologue," sniffed *USA Today*, "and made some cringingly bad pirate puns about hackers holding the new *Pirates Of The Caribbean* film hostage for ransom."

"STYLES GAVE A DEADPAN MONOLOGUE AND MADE SOME CRINGINGLY BAD PIRATE PUNS"

© Getty

LIGHTS UP

Performing on his first solo headline tour, Harry holds New York's iconic Madison Square Garden spellbound on 21 June 2018. The 20,000-capacity venue was treated to cuts from the singer's first solo album, crowd-pleasers from the One Direction era, plus covers of Fleetwood Mac and Ariana Grande. "He's the ultimate fusion of Mick Jagger's yin and Paul McCartney's yang," wrote Rob Sheffield in a glowing review for *Rolling Stone*. "That mix of the Stonesy flamboyant rogue and the Beatlesy romantic charmer. He was determined to make you feel uplifted, no matter how low you felt when you walked in."

"HE'S THE ULTIMATE FUSION OF MICK JAGGER'S YIN AND PAUL MCCARTNEY'S YANG"

BEST OF FRIENDS

The 2019 Rock and Roll Hall of Fame Induction Ceremony was the setting for this live performance by Harry Styles and Stevie Nicks on 29 March. At the event, Styles inducted Nicks into the Rock and Roll Hall of Fame as a solo artist. The pair originally met in 2015 after a Fleetwood Mac concert and became close friends, first performing together on stage in May 2017. Nicks is a huge fan of his album *Fine Line* and has even likened it to Fleetwood Mac's seminal album *Rumours*. "I wrote him a letter that said, 'This is your *Rumours* so you have to really respect it and adore it because these kinds of records sometimes don't ever come again'," she explained.

FLOWER POWER

Harry arrives at the Met Gala Celebrating Camp: Notes on Fashion exhibition on 6 May 2019. Held at the Metropolitan Museum of Art in New York, the event explored "the origins of camp's exuberant aesthetic" through 250 objects spanning from the 17th century to the present day. Co-chairing the exhibition alongside Lady Gaga, Serena Williams and *Vogue* editor-in-chief Anna Wintour, Harry looked the part in a sheer ruffled blouse, painted nails, pearl earring and heels. "I think everyone was expecting Harry to be in sequins, bright colours and a crown," said the star's stylist Harry Lambert, "but we decided on a different type of 'camp'."

"EVERYONE WAS EXPECTING SEQUINS,
BRIGHT COLOURS AND A CROWN.
WE DECIDED ON A DIFFERENT 'CAMP'"

FASHION STATEMENT

Harry appears at New York's Metropolitan Museum Of Art to launch the Met Gala Celebrating Camp: Notes on Fashion exhibition with co-hosts Serena Williams, Alessandro Michele, Lady Gaga and Anna Wintour. Inspired by Susan Sontag's influential 1964 essay, *Notes on Camp*, the exhibition set out to "examine how the elements of irony, humour, parody, pastiche, artifice, theatricality and exaggeration are expressed in fashion", and proved a huge critical success. "The historical journey is thoroughly engaging," wrote *The New York Times*. "You don't stop thinking about it. It sticks with you and niggles in the brain."

C'EST CHIC

Kendall Jenner and Harry attend the annual high-profile gala at the Metropolitan Museum of Art, better known as the Met. The gala is widely regarded as New York's most exciting fashion event of the year, and in 2019 Harry embraced the theme as he made his pink carpet debut wearing an all-black custom Gucci outfit, a pearl earring and shiny black-heeled boots. "The look I feel is elegant. It's camp, but it's still Harry," said his stylist.

BALLIN' FOR BRITAIN

A focused Harry leads the 'UK' dodgeball team into battle against Michelle Obama's 'USA' side on the *Late, Late Show* in May 2019. Flanked by host James Corden, actors John Bradley and Benedict Cumberbatch, and comedian Reggie Watts (the team's 'undercover' American), Harry meant business. Unfortunately for the UK squad, so did the former First Lady's charges (comprising Melissa McCarthy, Kate Hudson, Mila Kunis, Lena Waithe and Alison Janney), and it was the USA who would emerge victorious, clinching the match two games to one and ultimately settling the all-important argument of 'which country is better'. Not that James Corden agreed...

"HARRY MEANT BUSINESS. UNFORTUNATELY, SO DID THE FIRST LADY'S CHARGES"

© Getty

THE LATE

HOST WITH THE MOST

Filling in for a second time as a guest host on *The Late Late Show* for longtime friend James Corden in 2019, Harry started the show with a Carpool Karaoke skit that saw Corden advising him to feign interest should a guest tell a boring story. The British comedian then scarpered, leaving Harry to host actress Tracee Ellis Ross and model Kendall Jenner. With his usual boyish charm, Harry cracked several jokes about Donald Trump's potential impeachment, poked fun at the Guinness World Records and informed Kris Jenner (sitting in a guest room with daughter Kendall) that her garish yellow coat looked like a cross between Big Bird and a fisherman's jacket. He then wrapped up with a performance of 'Adore You' from his new album *Fine Line*. When it comes to hosting, he's a bit of a natural.

83

FAN BOY

Harry prepares to welcome a handful of lucky fans to Spotify's exclusive listening party in Los Angeles on 11 December 2019, celebrating the imminent *Fine Line* album. With the entire building transformed into the fictional island of Eroda – complete with boats, fishermen and a sashimi buffet – the evening's entertainment included a beauty parlour, a puppet show, a first listen to *Fine Line* and an appearance by the superstar singer himself. "I couldn't be here without you," Harry told the intimate crowd, promising them tickets to his upcoming show at the Forum. "You gave me the environment I needed to create this."

BEATS ON THE BEACH

A beaming Harry performs alongside US chart-topper Lizzo on a Miami beach as part of a series of concerts hosted by SiriusXM in the run-up to the 2020 Super Bowl. After whipping up the crowd, Lizzo halted her performance to introduce a mystery guest to the audience. Out strolled Harry, clad in a typically unique cardigan, belting out the lyrics to 'Juice'. Needless to say, the crowd went wild as the pair continued to leap around the stage, backed by a host of dancers and inter-changing pink and blue lights.

"THE CROWD WENT WILD AS THE PAIR CONTINUED TO LEAP AROUND THE STAGE"

© Getty

HEART AND SOUL

The O2 Arena in London was the setting for this performance at the BRIT Awards 2020 on 18 February. Harry performed the soulful ballad 'Falling' on a stage covered in water, with more water flowing out of a grand piano. Harry told *Rolling Stone* magazine that he wrote "the dreamy soul ballad" when singer-songwriter and producer Tom 'Kid Harpoon' Hull came over to his house. "Tom had come up to my place to grab something, and he'd sat at the piano and I'd just got out of the shower," explained Harry. "He started playing, and we wrote it there." The song is believed to be a tribute to Harry's ex-girlfriend Caroline Flack.

> "HARRY PERFORMED THE SOULFUL BALLAD 'FALLING' ON A STAGE COVERED IN WATER, WITH MORE WATER FLOWING OUT OF A GRAND PIANO"

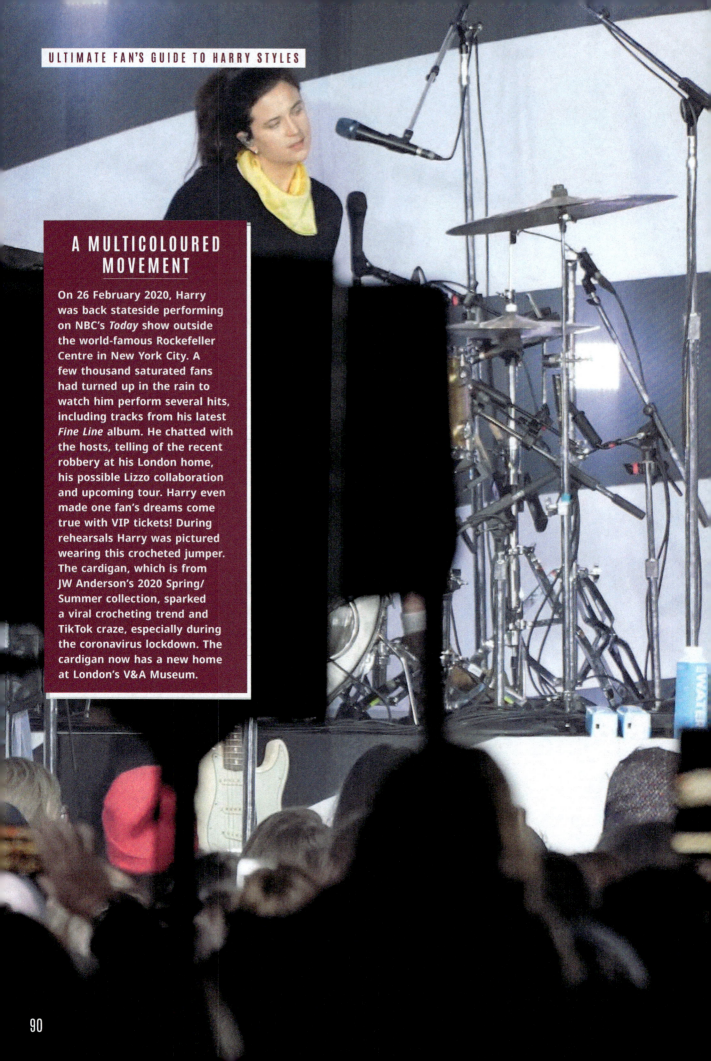

A MULTICOLOURED MOVEMENT

On 26 February 2020, Harry was back stateside performing on NBC's *Today* show outside the world-famous Rockefeller Centre in New York City. A few thousand saturated fans had turned up in the rain to watch him perform several hits, including tracks from his latest *Fine Line* album. He chatted with the hosts, telling of the recent robbery at his London home, his possible Lizzo collaboration and upcoming tour. Harry even made one fan's dreams come true with VIP tickets! During rehearsals Harry was pictured wearing this crocheted jumper. The cardigan, which is from JW Anderson's 2020 Spring/ Summer collection, sparked a viral crocheting trend and TikTok craze, especially during the coronavirus lockdown. The cardigan now has a new home at London's V&A Museum.

"HARRY'S CARDIGAN SPARKED A VIRAL CROCHETING TREND AND TIKTOK CRAZE, ESPECIALLY DURING LOCKDOWN"

¡HEART HARRY!

Performing at the iHeartRadio Secret Session at the Bowery Ballroom in New York City on 29 February 2020, Harry brought his charm and infectious energy to what was originally a secret event (details of the venue were not disclosed to fans until the day of the show). The star performed six songs, including favourites 'Kiwi', 'Watermelon Sugar' and 'Sign Of The Times', and took part in a candid Q&A. He rounded the night off by performing 'Falling', his newly announced single, the music video of which had been released earlier that week and was already a hit with his legion of followers.

TWINSET AND PEARLS

As the global pandemic hit, Harry Styles, like numerous artists and bands across the globe, was forced to cancel and postpone numerous shows as the reality of lockdown took hold. However, that didn't stop him from attending a secret radio session for SiriusXM's Hits 1 show in midtown Manhattan on 2 March 2020. Harry, who was resplendent in blue knitwear, lace collar and pearls, discussed the possibility of reuniting with One Direction via the medium of Zoom. He also updated fans on his 'Watermelon Sugar' music video and spoke about what he had been doing "stuck" in Los Angeles.

"HARRY, WHO WAS RESPLENDENT IN BLUE KNITWEAR, LACE COLLAR AND PEARLS, DISCUSSED THE POSSIBILITY OF REUNITING WITH ONE DIRECTION"

IF YOU'VE GOT IT, FLAUNT IT

Harry arrives at the 63rd Annual Grammy Awards at Los Angeles' Staples Center on 14 March 2021. Later in the ceremony, his smash hit 'Watermelon Sugar' would win Best Pop Solo Performance, marking Harry's first Grammy award. Stepping onto the podium in a mustard checked jacket and purple feather boa for his acceptance speech, the star praised fellow nominees Taylor Swift, Billie Eilish, Justin Bieber, Dua Lipa and Doja Cat but was bleeped out by squeamish US broadcasters for dropping the f-bomb ("I feel very grateful to be here… all these songs are f***ing massive").

"THE SONG'S HYPNOTIC GROOVE KICKED IN AS HARRY RIFFED AND GRINNED"

BACK IN BLACK

Harry opened the 63rd Grammy Awards with a sensual rendition of his hit number 'Watermelon Sugar'. From the first few bars, his voice sounded rich and assured against the minimal opening sounds of electric piano and trumpets. Fifty seconds into the performance the song's hypnotic groove kicked in as Harry riffed and grinned with his impressive band on the set's soundstage. He was dressed in matching black leather trousers and jacket and a feather boa. One minute and 50 seconds in, the bare-chested Styles tossed the feather boa aside, leaving him free to flaunt his tattoos as he rocked out through to the song's conclusion.

BEST OF BRITISH

Harry wins his second BRIT gong at the 2021 BRIT Awards, hosted at London's 02 Arena on 11 May, his catchy summer anthem 'Watermelon Sugar' netting him British Single of the year. The star turned heads by wearing a retro 1970s-style suit that he had previously worn a month prior on the Gucci runway. The dapper singer graciously accepted the award with a slight hint of an American accent in his acceptance speech. Fans were delighted by his appearance as he had not been seen before the show on the red carpet due to filming commitments.

"THE STAR TURNED HEADS BY WEARING A 1970S-STYLE SUIT THAT HE'D WORN A MONTH PRIOR ON THE GUCCI RUNWAY"

LOVE TRIANGLE

Harry in Brighton in May 2021 on the set of *My Policeman*, a romantic drama set in the 1950s and based on the novel by Bethan Roberts. Styles plays Tom, a gay police officer who is married to a school teacher called Marion (Emma Corrin) while also being in a relationship with a museum curator called Patrick (David Dawson). For a while the three characters embrace their lives as a ménage a trois, until jealousy shatters the relationship. The film, due for release in autumn 2022, highlights the restrictions placed on gay men at the time, when homosexuality was illegal in the UK.

© Getty

VIVA LAS VEGAS

Harry raises the roof of the MGM Grand Garden Arena during the opening show of Love On Tour on 4 September 2021. Having twice postponed the tour due to the coronavirus pandemic, the singer pulled out all the stops in Las Vegas, taking to the stage in a pink fringed vest, airing almost all the songs from his *Fine Line* album, flying the Pride flag, and politely asking his fans to stay masked while in the building. "I know things are a bit different," he explained. "[But] I've always found that you can tell the most about a person from their eyes anyway."

"THE SINGER PULLED OUT
ALL THE STOPS IN LAS VEGAS"

HARRYWEEN HIGH

Anticipation was high when Harry announced his two-night 'Harryween' fancy dress party at New York's Madison Square Garden on 30 October 2021. He didn't disappoint. His fans, known as 'Stylers', took him up on his challenge to dress up for the occasion while he – not too surprisingly – made his own distinct sartorial statement. On the first of the two nights he emerged onstage as Dorothy from the *Wizard Of Oz*, kitted out in a blue-and-white gingham dress with a white collar and red hearts. The outfit was finished off with red tights and Dorothy's renowned ruby slippers.

© Getty

SEND IN THE CLOWNS

Harry performs on the second night of 'Harryween' at Madison Square Garden on 31 October 2021. The singer encouraged fans to come in fancy dress and led by example, arriving onstage in a Gucci clown suit that reminded some commentators of David Bowie's outfit from the classic *Ashes To Ashes* video. "Styles is known for engaging with his audience, and I was not disappointed," wrote *Insider*'s reviewer. "He made a point to move around the entire stage and pay attention to each area in the crowd. The joy and gratitude in the room were palpable, including and especially from Styles himself, who hardly stopped grinning."

GOING, GOING, GONE!

Laid out in a brightly lit display room in Los Angeles, an array of instruments and other memorabilia once belonging to a host of stars await an auction that will draw bidders from around the globe. Hosted by Julian's Auctions, an organisation that sells rare pop culture memorabilia in order to raise funds for numerous charities, this collection included guitars signed by Harry Styles, Machine Gun Kelly, Paul McCartney, Metallica, Tom Petty, Slash, Keith Richards and Depeche Mode. Also on display is an elaborate white dress formerly worn by Katy Perry and a jacket that once belonged to Lionel Richie.

WILDE FOR EACH OTHER

Harry and girlfriend Olivia Wilde are spotted out in Soho, London, Soho, on 15 March 2022. The undeniable power couple even sported coordinating outfits as they enjoyed some casual weekday shopping close to where Harry opened his Pleasing pop-up shop the previous week. Olivia and Harry both share a love and appreciation for style and fashion that is a thread throughout the film *Don't Worry, Darling*, which was directed by Wilde. The couple met on set, Harry perfectly cast given his passion for fashion and unique designs.

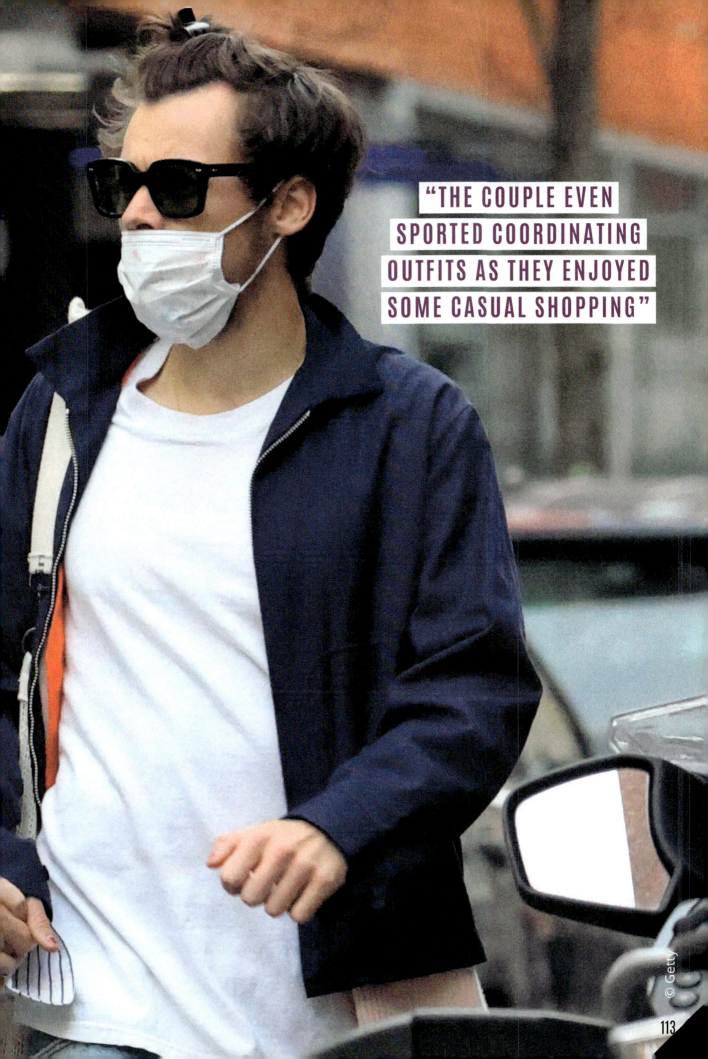

"THE COUPLE EVEN SPORTED COORDINATING OUTFITS AS THEY ENJOYED SOME CASUAL SHOPPING"

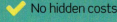 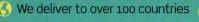